TABLE OF

GW01315774

TABLE OF CONTENTS

Good luck Best wishes
Dom

Good luck,
Nice to meet you.

Matt.

Josh, it's been lovely to have you part of our team! Good luck with your adventures. Terhi from ABI therapy team

Good luck Josh! Don't think I'll bump into you in Australia! All the best, Ellen
(OT Apprentice)

Good luck, Josh
You've been great to work with.
Best wishes
Sharon

Good Luck in Australia Josh.
Good to work with you.
Nicole.

Good luck with your adventures in Australia! Ellie

INTRODUCTION

G'day, mate! If you're reading this, you're probably getting ready to dive into the wonderful, weird, and wildly entertaining world of Australian slang. Whether you're visiting Down Under, planning to mingle with some Aussies, or just curious about what phrases like "fair dinkum" or "spit the dummy" mean, you've come to the right place.

This book is your ultimate guide to sounding like a local—or at least understanding what on earth the locals are saying. Aussies are known for their love of abbreviations, humour, and laid-back vibes, and their slang reflects all of that. Trust me, once you start throwing words like "ripper" or "snag" into conversation, you'll be hooked.

Here's how I've structured the book to make it fun and easy for you to learn:

1. Thematic Sections:

- I've grouped slang into themes, like everyday chat, food and gatherings, beach slang, and Aussie humour. This way, you can focus on the phrases you'll actually need in different situations, whether you're at a barbie, at the beach, or just chatting with mates.

2. Alphabetical Glossary:

- After the themed sections, you'll find a full A-to-Z glossary for quick reference. Think of it as your slang dictionary when you need to decode something on the spot.

And because we know learning slang should be fun, I've thrown in some cheeky jokes, common tourist mistakes, and quirky illustrations to keep you entertained along the way.

By the end of this book, you'll not only understand Aussie slang but also the culture behind it. You'll sound more like a true blue Aussie and less like a confused tourist scratching your head at phrases like, "Chuck a sickie" or "Rack off." So, grab a cuppa, settle in, and get ready to have a ripper time learning the language of the Land Down Under.

Let's get started!

EXCLUSIF BONUSES

BONUS 1: CHEAT SHEET TOP 50 MUST-KNOW SLANG

Terms Keep this handy guide in your pocket for quick reference. From "G'day" to "Fair dinkum," this cheat sheet covers the essentials that'll have you sounding like a true-blue Aussie in no time.

BONUS 2: ADVANCED SLANG FOR THE TRUE BLUE LEGENDS

Think you've got what it takes to hang with the pros? This bonus section is your ticket to mastering advanced Aussie slang that'll impress even the locals.

EVERYDAY AUSSIE

Ready to chat like a local? This section is packed with everyday phrases Aussies drop into conversation without a second thought. Whether you're saying "G'day" or telling someone "No worries," you'll sound like a natural in no time. Keep it relaxed, keep it fun —just like the Aussies do!

G'DAY

GUH-DAY

 DEFINITION

A friendly way to say "hello" or "good day."

 EXAMPLE

"G'DAY, MATE!"

"G'DAY! HOW YA GOIN'?"

HOW YA GOIN'?

HOW YA GO-IN

 DEFINITION

A casual way to ask, "How are you?"

 EXAMPLE

"G'DAY, SHEILA! HOW YA GOIN'?"

"NOT BAD, MATE. YOURSELF?"

HOOROO

HOO-ROO

DEFINITION

A casual way to say "goodbye."

EXAMPLE

"ALRIGHT, I BETTER HEAD OFF. HOOROO!"

"HOOROO, MATE! SEE YA NEXT TIME."

GOOD ON YA

GOOD ON YA

DEFINITION

"Well done" or "good for you."

EXAMPLE

"I FINALLY GOT THE JOB!"

"GOOD ON YA, MATE!"

CHEERS

CHEERS

📖 DEFINITION

Used to say "thank you," "goodbye," or as a toast.

💬 EXAMPLE

"HERE'S YOUR COFFEE."

"CHEERS, MATE!"

TA TA

TAH-TAH

📖 DEFINITION

An informal way to say "bye-bye."

💬 EXAMPLE

"ALRIGHT, I'LL SEE YOU TOMORROW. TA TA!"

"TA TA, MATE!"

NO WORRIES

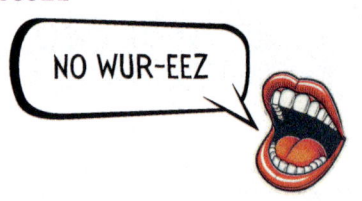 NO WUR-EEZ

DEFINITION

"It's okay," "no problem," or "don't worry about it."

EXAMPLE

 "SORRY I'M LATE!"

"NO WORRIES, MATE. IT HAPPENS!"

SHE'LL BE RIGHT

 SHEEL BE RAHT

DEFINITION

"It will be okay" or "everything will work out."

EXAMPLE

 "I'M WORRIED ABOUT THE PROJECT DEADLINE."

"DON'T STRESS. SHE'LL BE RIGHT, MATE!"

WHAT'S CRACKIN'?

WOTS KRACK-IN

DEFINITION

A casual greeting similar to "What's up?"

EXAMPLE

"G'DAY, MATE! WHAT'S CRACKIN'?"

"NOT MUCH, JUST FINISHED BREKKIE."

WHAT'S THE GO?

WOTS THE GO?

DEFINITION

"What's happening?" or "What's going on?"

EXAMPLE

"WHAT'S THE GO WITH THE FOOTY MATCH TONIGHT?"

"IT STARTS AT 7, MATE."

FAIR DINKUM

FAIR DINK-UM

DEFINITION

"True," "real," or "genuine."

EXAMPLE

"DID YOU SEE A KOALA IN THE WILD?"

"FAIR DINKUM, MATE! IT WAS RIGHT THERE IN THE TREE."

I RECKON..

EYE RECK-ON

DEFINITION

"I think" or "I believe."

EXAMPLE

"IS IT GOING TO RAIN TODAY?"

"I RECKON IT MIGHT, BETTER TAKE A BROLLY."

BLOODY OATH

BLUD-EE OATH

DEFINITION

That's certainly true; used to strongly agree.

EXAMPLE

"THIS BARBIE'S GOT THE BEST SNAGS IN TOWN!"

"BLOODY OATH, MATE!"

BLOODY

BLUD-EE

DEFINITION

Used to emphasise something (e.g., very).

EXAMPLE

"THAT WAS BLOODY HARD YAKKA TODAY."

"YEAH, MATE, I'M KNACKERED!"

13

HEAPS

HEEPS

 DEFINITION

A lot or many.

 EXAMPLE

"THERE ARE HEAPS OF MOZZIES OUT TONIGHT."

"BETTER SLAP ON SOME REPELLENT!"

GIVE IT A BURL

GIV IT UH BERL

 DEFINITION

To try something or have a go.

 EXAMPLE

"I'VE NEVER SURFED BEFORE."

"NO WORRIES, MATE. JUST GIVE IT A BURL!"

14

TOO RIGHT

 TOO RIGHT

📖 DEFINITION

Definitely or absolutely.

💬 EXAMPLE

 *"THIS PUB GRUB IS TOP-NOTCH."*

"TOO RIGHT, MATE!"

NO DRAMA

 NO DRAH-MAH

📖 DEFINITION

Same as "no worries"; it's okay or don't stress.

💬 EXAMPLE

 *"SORRY ABOUT THE MIX-UP EARLIER."*

"NO DRAMA, MATE. HAPPENS TO EVERYONE."

TRUE BLUE

TROO BLOO

 DEFINITION

Patriotic or genuinely Australian.

 EXAMPLE

"HE'S BEEN WORKING ON THE STATION FOR 30 YEARS."

"TRUE BLUE AUSSIE THROUGH AND THROUGH!"

"DON'T SAY 'G'DAY, MATE!' TO EVERYONE. IT'S SUPER CASUAL—STICK TO FRIENDS OR LAID-BACK SITUATIONS. SAYING IT TO YOUR BOSS? AWKWARD."

FOOD, DRINKS, AND GATHERINGS

Aussies love their grub, and they've got some of the most unique (and delicious) ways of talking about it. From throwing snags on the barbie to grabbing a choccy biccy with your cuppa, this section will have you chatting like a pro at any meal, barbecue, or pub gathering. Get your appetite ready—it's going to be a ripper!

17

BREKKIE

BREK-EE

 DEFINITION

Breakfast, the first meal of the day.

 EXAMPLE

"WHAT'S FOR BREKKIE THIS MORNING?"

"JUST SOME TOAST AND AVO, MATE."

SANGA

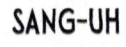

SANG-UH

 DEFINITION

A sandwich, typically a simple one.

 EXAMPLE

"I'M STARVING. LET'S GRAB A SANGA."

"GOOD IDEA, MATE. I KNOW A GREAT CAFE NEARBY."

SMOH-KOH

DEFINITION

A short break during work, often for tea or snacks.

EXAMPLE

"TIME FOR SMOKO, LET'S GRAB A PIE."

"SOUNDS GOOD, MATE. MEET YOU BY THE UTE."

KUP-UH

DEFINITION

A cup of tea (sometimes coffee).

EXAMPLE

"FANCY A CUPPA?"

"YEAH, A CUPPA WOULD BE GREAT RIGHT NOW."

TEA

TEE

DEFINITION

Dinner or the evening meal in some regions.

EXAMPLE

"WHAT'S FOR TEA TONIGHT?"

"WE'RE HAVING ROAST CHOOK AND VEG."

SPAG BOL

SPAG BOL

DEFINITION

Spaghetti Bolognese, a pasta dish with meat sauce.

EXAMPLE

"I'M MAKING SPAG BOL FOR DINNER."

"YUM! I'LL BE OVER AT 7!"

CHOCCY BICCY

CHOK-EE BIK-EE

 DEFINITION

A chocolate biscuit (cookie).

 EXAMPLE

"I ALWAYS HAVE A CHOCCY BICCY WITH MY TEA."

"SAME HERE. TIM TAMS ARE MY FAVOURITE!"

FAIRY BREAD

FAIR-EE BRED

 DEFINITION

White bread with butter and sprinkles, a kid's treat.

 EXAMPLE

"LET'S MAKE FAIRY BREAD FOR THE PARTY."

"PERFECT. THE KIDS WILL LOVE IT!"

SNAG

SNAG

 DEFINITION

A sausage, often grilled or fried.

 EXAMPLE

"THROW A FEW SNAGS ON THE BARBIE."

"ALRIGHT, MATE. YOU BRING THE BREAD ROLLS."

SAUSAGE SIZZLE

SOS-IJ SIZZ-UHL

 DEFINITION

A sausage cooked on a BBQ, often sold at fundraisers.

 EXAMPLE

"THERE'S A SAUSAGE SIZZLE AT THE SHOPS."

"GREAT, I'LL GRAB A SNAG ON BREAD."

LAMINGTONS

LAM-ING-TUNZ

DEFINITION

Sponge cake squares with chocolate icing and coconut.

EXAMPLE

"I BROUGHT LAMINGTONS FOR AFTERNOON TEA."

"CHEERS! THEY LOOK AMAZING."

PAVLOVA

PAV-LOH-VUH

DEFINITION

A meringue dessert topped with cream and fruit.

EXAMPLE

"I MADE PAVLOVA FOR DESSERT TONIGHT."

"DELICIOUS! IT'S MY FAVOURITE AUSSIE TREAT."

CHOOK

CHOOK

 **DEFINITION**

A chicken, typically roast or grilled.

 **EXAMPLE**

"WE'RE HAVING ROAST
CHOOK FOR DINNER."

"I'LL MAKE THE GRAVY,
THEN!"

STUBBIE

STUB-EE

 **DEFINITION**

A small bottle of beer, usually 375ml.

 **EXAMPLE**

"GRAB A COUPLE OF
STUBBIES FOR THE BARBY."

"RIGHTO, MATE. I'LL GET
SOME FROM THE BOTTLE-O."

BARBY

BAR-BEE

DEFINITION

Barbecue, a social event where food is grilled outdoors.

EXAMPLE

"WE'RE HAVING A BARBY THIS WEEKEND."

"SWEET, I'LL BRING THE SNAGS AND A FEW BEERS."

PUB GRUB

PUB GRUB

DEFINITION

Food served in a pub, often hearty and filling.

EXAMPLE

"LET'S GRAB SOME PUB GRUB TONIGHT."

"GOOD IDEA. I COULD GO FOR A PARMI."

SHOUT

SHOWT

DEFINITION

To buy a round of drinks for a group.

EXAMPLE

"IT'S YOUR SHOUT, MATE."

"NO WORRIES, WHAT'S EVERYONE HAVING?"

BYO

BEE-WHY-OH

DEFINITION

Bring Your Own (alcohol) to a venue or event.

EXAMPLE

"IT'S A BYO PLACE, DON'T FORGET WINE."

"GOT IT! I'LL BRING A COUPLE OF BOTTLES."

ARVO

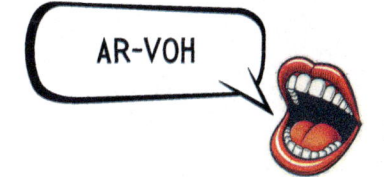

AR-VOH

DEFINITION

Afternoon.

EXAMPLE

"LET'S MEET UP THIS ARVO FOR A COFFEE."

"SOUNDS GOOD, SEE YOU AT 3!"

BIKKIE

BIK-EE

DEFINITION

Biscuit (cookie).

EXAMPLE

"I'M HAVING A BIKKIE WITH MY TEA."

"PASS ME A CHOCCY BIKKIE TOO!"

CUT LUNCH

KUT LUNCH

📖 DEFINITION

Sandwiches, usually packed to go.

💬 EXAMPLE

"I'VE GOT SOME CUT LUNCH IN MY TUCKERBOX."

"CHEERS! SANDWICHES WILL HIT THE SPOT."

BOG IN

BOG IN

📖 DEFINITION

To start eating enthusiastically.

💬 EXAMPLE

"DINNER'S READY, BOG IN, EVERYONE!"

"THANKS, MATE. SMELLS AMAZING!"

28

PASH

PASH

📖 DEFINITION

A long, passionate kiss.

💬 EXAMPLE

"DID YOU SEE THEM HAVE A PASH AT THE PARTY?"

"YEAH, THEY COULDN'T STOP!"

ESKY

ES-KEE

📖 DEFINITION

An insulated cooler for food and drinks.

💬 EXAMPLE

"I'LL GRAB THE BEERS FROM THE ESKY."

"MAKE SURE THEY'RE COLD, MATE!"

29

PREZZY

PREZ-EE

DEFINITION

A present or gift.

EXAMPLE

"WHAT PREZZY ARE YOU GETTING FOR HER BIRTHDAY?"

"PROBABLY A NICE BOTTLE OF WINE."

SANGER

SANG-UH

DEFINITION

A sandwich (regional variation of "sanga").

EXAMPLE

"I'M STARVING, LET'S GRAB A SANGER."

"GOOD IDEA, MATE. I FEEL LIKE HAM AND CHEESE."

TUCKER

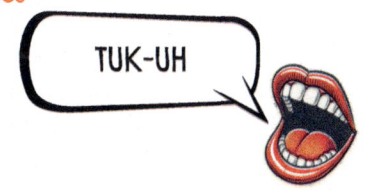

TUK-UH

DEFINITION

Food in general.

EXAMPLE

"THERE'S PLENTY OF TUCKER AT THE BARBIE."

"SWEET, I'LL GRAB A PLATE!"

TUCKERBOX

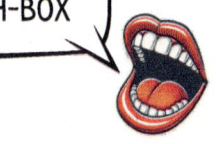

TUK-UH-BOX

DEFINITION

A lunch container or picnic box.

EXAMPLE

"I PACKED SANDWICHES IN THE TUCKERBOX."

"CHEERS, MATE. LOOKS LIKE A GOOD FEED!"

BEACH SLANG

Australia's beaches are world-famous, and so is the slang that comes with them! Whether you're catching a gnarly wave, slapping on some zinc, or spotting a few surfies, this section will have you sounding like a local in no time. Dive in and soak up the lingo—just watch out for the salties!

RIPPER

RIP-UH

DEFINITION

Something fantastic or excellent.

EXAMPLE

"THAT WAS A RIPPER OF A WAVE!"

"YEAH, MATE, YOU ABSOLUTELY NAILED IT!"

GNARLY

NAR-LEE

DEFINITION

Dangerous or challenging, often used for waves.

EXAMPLE

"THE SURF'S LOOKING GNARLY TODAY."

"ONLY THE PROS SHOULD BE OUT THERE!"

RASHIE

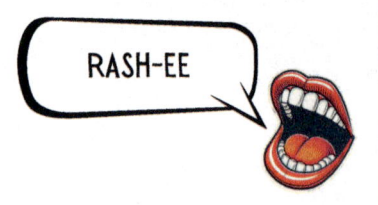 RASH-EE

DEFINITION

A rash guard shirt worn for sun protection or to prevent rashes.

EXAMPLE

 "DON'T FORGET YOUR RASHIE, IT'S SUNNY."

"THANKS, MATE. I'LL GRAB IT FROM THE CAR."

BEACHIES

 BEECH-EEZ

DEFINITION

Waves that break on a sandy beach, often gentler.

EXAMPLE

 "I PREFER SURFING BEACHIES, NOT REEFS."

"SAME HERE. IT'S EASIER WHEN YOU'RE LEARNING."

34

NIPPERS

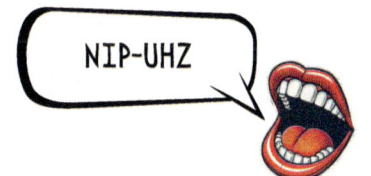

NIP-UHZ

DEFINITION

Children in a junior surf lifesaving program.

EXAMPLE

"MY KIDS ARE JOINING THE NIPPERS TODAY."

"GREAT, THEY'LL LEARN HEAPS ABOUT BEACH SAFETY!"

ZINC
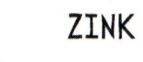

ZINK

DEFINITION

Sunscreen worn on the face, often in bright colours.

EXAMPLE

"PUT ON SOME ZINC BEFORE YOU BURN."

"GOOD CALL, I'VE GOT BRIGHT BLUE TODAY!"

SHARKY

SHAHR-KEE

 DEFINITION

Nervous or anxious about sharks in the water.

 EXAMPLE

"I FEEL A BIT SHARKY IN THIS MURKY WATER."

"DON'T WORRY, MATE. WE'RE IN A SAFE ZONE."

CLUBBIE

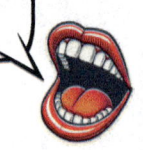

KLUB-EE

 DEFINITION

A member of a Surf Life Saving Club.

 EXAMPLE

"HE'S A DEDICATED CLUBBIE, ALWAYS PATROLLING."

"YEAH, HE'S BEEN A LIFESAVER FOR YEARS."

GROMMET

 GROM-IT

DEFINITION

A young or beginner surfer.

EXAMPLE

"THE GROMMETS ARE OUT CATCHING WAVES."

"THEY'RE DOING GREAT FOR BEGINNERS!"

SALTIE

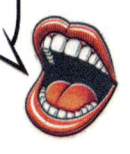 SAWL-TEE

DEFINITION

A saltwater crocodile, common in northern Australia.

EXAMPLE

"BE CAREFUL SWIMMING; THERE MIGHT BE SALTIES."

"YEAH, MATE, I'M STAYING WELL AWAY!"

BARREL

 BA-RUHL

DEFINITION

The hollow part of a wave that a surfer can ride inside.

EXAMPLE

 "I GOT BARRELED ON THAT LAST WAVE!"

"MATE, THAT'S THE DREAM!"

KOOK

 KOOK

DEFINITION

A surfer who's inexperienced or lacks etiquette.

EXAMPLE

 "THAT GUY'S SUCH A KOOK, HE'S DROPPING IN!"

"YEAH, HE NEEDS TO LEARN SOME SURF RULES."

WIPEOUT

WIPE-OUT

DEFINITION

Falling off a surfboard, often in dramatic fashion.

EXAMPLE

"SHE HAD A GNARLY WIPEOUT ON THAT WAVE."

"YEAH, BUT SHE POPPED BACK UP LIKE A PRO!"

"NEVER CALL YOUR FLIP-FLOPS 'SANDALS.' THEY'RE THONGS HERE, MATE! BUT BE CAREFUL WITH THAT WORD BACK HOME!"

THANK YOU SO MUCH
FOR MAKING IT THIS FAR!

Thank you so much for picking up my book! I'm thrilled to have been part of your journey into the fun and quirky world of Aussie slang.

If you enjoyed the book *(or even had a laugh or two along the way)*, I'd be incredibly grateful if you could **leave a review on Amazon**. Your feedback not only helps me grow but also helps other readers discover the book.

Here's how you can leave your review:
1. **Open your camera** app on your phone.
2. **Point it** at the QR code below.
3. **Follow the link** to the review page.

SCAN ME

Thanks again, and I hope you have a ripper time mastering Aussie lingo!

AUSSIE HUMOUR

Aussies have a knack for mixing sharp wit with playful jabs, and their slang is no exception. Whether it's calling someone a galah, pulling your head in, or joking about kangaroos in the top paddock, this section will have you laughing—and maybe scratching your head. Master these phrases, and you'll fit right in with the cheeky Aussie banter!

GALAH

GUH-LAH

DEFINITION

A fool or silly person.

EXAMPLE

"HE FELL FOR THE SAME TRICK TWICE!"

"WHAT A GALAH!"

RATBAG

RAT-BAG

DEFINITION

A mild insult for someone mischievous or unruly.

EXAMPLE

"THAT KID KEEPS STEALING BISCUITS."

"WHAT A LITTLE RATBAG!"

WHACKER

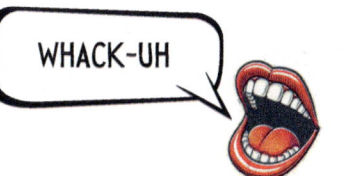 WHACK-UH

 ## DEFINITION

An idiot or fool.

 ## EXAMPLE

"HE TRIED TO SURF DURING A STORM."

"WHAT A WHACKER!"

FURPHY

 FUR-FEE

 ## DEFINITION

A false or unreliable rumour.

 ## EXAMPLE

"I HEARD THE OFFICE IS GETTING A POOL TABLE!"

"NAH, MATE, THAT'S JUST A FURPHY."

MATILDA

 MUH-TIL-DUH

 DEFINITION

Swagman's bedding; often a reference to "Waltzing Matilda."

 EXAMPLE

"HE PACKED HIS MATILDA AND WENT BUSH."

"CLASSIC AUSSIE ADVENTURE!"

RIP SNORTER

 RIP-SNORT-UH

 DEFINITION

Something great, fantastic, or excellent.

 EXAMPLE

"THAT PARTY WAS A RIP SNORTER!"

"YEAH, MATE, BEST NIGHT EVER!"

SPRUNG

SPRUNG

 **DEFINITION**

Caught doing something wrong.

 **EXAMPLE**

"I GOT SPRUNG SNEAKING INTO THE FOOTY GAME."

"SHOULD'VE BOUGHT A TICKET, MATE."

WHINGE

WINJ

 **DEFINITION**

To complain, often excessively.

 **EXAMPLE**

"STOP WHINGING ABOUT THE WEATHER!"

"I CAN'T HELP IT, MATE. IT'S FREEZING!"

TAKING THE PISS

TAYK-ING THE PISS

 DEFINITION

To make fun of someone in a playful way.

 EXAMPLE

"I RECKON I COULD OUTRUN A KANGAROO."

"YOU'RE TAKING THE PISS, MATE!"

CRACK A FAT

KRACK UH FAT

 DEFINITION

To get angry or upset.

 EXAMPLE

"THE WAITER FORGOT MY ORDER AGAIN!"

"NO NEED TO CRACK A FAT OVER IT, MATE."

46

SPIT THE DUMMY

SPIT THUH DUM-EE

 DEFINITION

To throw a tantrum or overreact dramatically.

 EXAMPLE

"HE DIDN'T GET HIS WAY, SO HE SPAT THE DUMMY."

"CLASSIC! HE'S ALWAYS OVERREACTING."

PULL YOUR HEAD IN

PULL YOR HED IN

 DEFINITION

A phrase telling someone to stop acting foolishly or being over the top.

 EXAMPLE

"I'M GOING TO BUY A FERRARI NEXT WEEK!"

"PULL YOUR HEAD IN, MATE. THAT'S NOT HAPPENING."

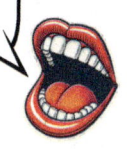

STIR THE POSSUM

STUR THUH POSS-UM

 DEFINITION

To provoke or agitate someone for amusement.

 EXAMPLE

"I TOLD HIM HIS TEAM WAS RUBBISH."

"YOU'RE JUST TRYING TO STIR THE POSSUM, AREN'T YOU?"

PIECE OF PISS

PEESS OV PISS

 DEFINITION

Something very easy or simple to do.

 EXAMPLE

"HOW WAS THE EXAM?"

"PIECE OF PISS, MATE!"

DEADSET

DED-SET

DEFINITION

Absolutely true or definite.

EXAMPLE

"DID YOU REALLY SEE A KOALA IN YOUR BACKYARD?"

"DEADSET, MATE. IT WAS JUST CHILLING IN THE TREE!"

BUCKLEY'S CHANCE

BUCK-LEEZ CHANSS

DEFINITION

No chance at all; very slim odds.

EXAMPLE

"DO YOU THINK WE'LL WIN THE LOTTERY?"

"BUCKLEY'S CHANCE, MATE, BUT WORTH A SHOT!"

YOU'RE DREAMIN'

YOR DREAM-IN

 DEFINITION

A response to someone being unrealistic or delusional.

 EXAMPLE

"I'LL ASK THE BOSS FOR A THREE-MONTH HOLIDAY."

"YOU'RE DREAMIN', MATE!"

NOT THE FULL QUID

NOT THUH FULL KWID

 DEFINITION

Refers to someone who's not very intelligent or a bit crazy.

EXAMPLE

"HE WENT SWIMMING WITH HIS PHONE IN HIS POCKET."

"YEAH, HE'S NOT THE FULL QUID, IS HE?"

DON'T COME THE RAW PRAWN WITH ME

DOH-NT KUM THUH RAW PRAWN WITH MEE

📖 DEFINITION

Don't try to fool or deceive me.

💬 EXAMPLE

"I SWEAR I DIDN'T BREAK IT!"

"DON'T COME THE RAW PRAWN WITH ME, I SAW YOU!"

KANGAROOS LOOSE IN THE TOP PADDOCK

KANG-UH-ROOS LOOSE IN THUH TOP PAD-UK

📖 DEFINITION

A humorous way to say someone's a bit crazy.

💬 EXAMPLE

"HE SAID HE COULD TALK TO ALIENS!"

"SOUNDS LIKE HE'S GOT KANGAROOS LOOSE IN THE TOP PADDOCK."

CHUCK A WOBBLY

 CHUK UH WOB-LEE

DEFINITION

To throw a tantrum or get upset in an exaggerated way.

EXAMPLE

"HE CHUCKED A WOBBLY WHEN HIS TOAST BURNED."

"THAT'S OVER THE TOP, MATE!"

WALKABOUT

WALK-UH-BOUT

DEFINITION

Lost or can't be found (often used humorously).

EXAMPLE

"WHERE'S YOUR PHONE?"

"GONE WALKABOUT AGAIN, MATE!"

52

THE ULTIMATE AUSSIE SLANG GLOSSARY

Welcome to the ultimate Aussie slang cheat sheet! This alphabetical glossary is your go-to guide for quickly looking up any slang word you've heard or want to try out. Whether you're brushing up before a trip, decoding what the locals are saying, or just having a laugh at the lingo, this section has got you covered.

Each entry is short and snappy, with an easy pronunciation guide, a quick definition, and an example to help you use it like a pro. Flip through, find your favourites, and have fun talking like a true blue Aussie!

GLOSSARY
A

ACE
AYSS

 Excellent or very good.

"That was an ace performance, mate!"

ANKLE BITER
AN-KUL BYE-TUH

 A small child.

"My ankle biters are running wild today."

APPLES, SHE'LL BE
AP-UHLS, SHEEL BEE

 It'll be all right or everything will work out.

"Don't worry about the test, she'll be apples."

ARVO
AR-VOH

 Afternoon.

"Let's grab a coffee this arvo."

AUSSIE SALUTE
OZ-EE SUH-LOOT

 Brushing flies away with your hand.

"I spent all day doing the Aussie salute out bush."

WHY DID THE KANGAROO STOP DRINKING COFFEE? BECAUSE IT MADE HIM TOO JUMPY!

BACK OF BOURKE

BAK OV BURK

A very remote or distant place.

"He lives way out the back of Bourke."

BARBY

BAR-BEE

A barbecue or grill.

"We're having a barby this weekend."

BIG SMOKE

BIG SMOAK

A big city, like Sydney or Melbourne.

"I'm heading to the big smoke tomorrow."

BIKKIE

BIK-EE

A biscuit (cookie).

"I'm having a cuppa and a bikkie."

BILLABONG

BIL-UH-BONG

A waterhole or oxbow lake.

"We swam in the billabong to cool off."

BLOKE

BLOHK

A man or guy.

"That bloke over there is a legend!"

GLOSSARY

 BLOODY
BLUD-EE

 Very (used for emphasis).

 "It's bloody hot today!"

BARBY
BAR-BEE

 That's absolutely true.

 "That concert was amazing!"   "Bloody oath, mate!"

 BLOWIE
BLOW-EE

 A blow fly.

 "The blowies were everywhere at the picnic."

BLUDGER
BLUD-JUH

 A lazy person.

 "He's such a bludger, always skipping work."

BOG IN
BOG IN

 To start eating enthusiastically.

 "Dinner's ready, so bog in!"

BONZER
BONZ-UH

 Great or excellent.

 "That was a bonzer effort, mate!"

GLOSSARY

BOTTLER

BOT-LUH

 Something exceptional or great.

 "That idea is an absolute bottler!"

BREKKIE

BREK-EE

 Breakfast

 "Let's grab some brekkie before heading out."

BUSH TELLY

BUSH TEL-EE

 A campfire.

 "We sat around the bush telly last night."

BYO

BEE-WHY-OH

 Bring your own (alcohol or food).

 "The party's BYO, so grab some beers."

WHY DON'T AUSSIES PLAY HIDE AND SEEK? BECAUSE GOOD LUCK HIDING WHEN YOU'RE ALWAYS SAYING, 'COOEE!'

GLOSSARY

C

CACTUS

KAK-TUS

 Dead, broken, or not working.

 "My phone's cactus after I dropped it."

CHOOK

CHOOK

 A chicken.

"We're having roast chook for dinner."

CHOCCY BICCY

CHOK-EE BIK-EE

 A chocolate biscuit (cookie).

 "Pass me a choccy biccy with my tea."

CLUBBIE

KLUB-EE

 A member of a surf lifesaving club.

 "That clubbie saved someone from a rip."

COZZIE

KOZ-EE

 A swimming costume.

 "Don't forget your cozzie for the beach."

CRACK A FAT

KRACK UH FAT

 To get angry or upset.

 "No need to crack a fat, mate."

CRANKY
KRANG-KEE

 Irritable or in a bad mood.

 "She's cranky because she didn't sleep well."

CROOK
KRUK

 Sick or unwell.

 "I'm feeling a bit crook today."

CUT LUNCH
KUT LUNCH

 Sandwiches, typically packed to go.

 "We packed some cut lunch for the road trip."

DAG
DAG

 A person who's a bit uncool but endearing.

 "He's such a dag with his dad jokes."

DAKS
DAKS

 Trousers or pants.

 "Those are some fancy daks you're wearing!"

DEADSET
DED-SET

 Absolutely true or definite.

 "Deadset, that was the best barbie ever."

DIPSTICK
DIP-STIK

 A silly or foolish person.

 "Stop being a dipstick and focus, mate!"

DON'T COME THE RAW PRAWN

 Don't try to fool me.

 "Don't come the raw prawn, I know what you did!"

DOWN UNDER
DOW-N UN-DUH

 A nickname for Australia.

 "Welcome to Down Under, mate!"

DROVER
DROH-VUH

 A person who herds cattle or sheep.

 "The drovers are leading the herd today."

DUNNY
DUN-EE

 A toilet, often outdoors.

 "I need to find a dunny real quick!"

E

EARBASHING

EER-BASH-ING

 Excessive talking or nagging.

 "He gave me an earbashing about being late."

ESKY

ES-KEE

 An insulated food/drink cooler.

 "Grab a cold drink from the esky, mate."

FAIRY BREAD

FAIR-EE BRED

 White bread with butter and sprinkles.

 "We made fairy bread for the kids' party."

FAIR DINKUM

FAIR DINK-UM

 Genuine, true, or sincere.

 "Fair dinkum, mate, that was incredible!"

FAIR GO

FAIR GO

A chance or an opportunity.

 "Everyone deserves a fair go in life."

GLOSSARY

FOOTY

FOOT-EE

 Australian Rules football.

 "Are you watching the footy this weekend?"

FULL

FULL

 Drunk or intoxicated.

 "He was so full after all those beers."

FURPHY

FUR-FEE

 A false or unreliable rumour.

 "That story about free beer was a furphy!"

G'DAY

GUH-DAY

 A friendly greeting meaning "hello."

 "G'day, mate! How's it going?"

GALAH

GUH-LAH

 A fool or silly person.

 "He's acting like a total galah today."

GIVE IT A BURL

GIV IT UH BERL

 To give something a try.

 "Never surfed before? Just give it a burl!"

GLOSSARY

GNARLY
NAR-LEE

 Dangerous or impressive, often about waves.

 "The surf looks gnarly today, be careful!"

GOOD ON YA
GOOD ON YA

 Well done or good for you.

 "You finished the race? Good on ya, mate!"

GRAND FINAL
GRAND FYE-NUHL

 The championship game in a sporting season.

 "Are you going to watch the grand final?"

GROMMET
GROM-IT

 A young or beginner surfer.

 "The grommets are out catching their first waves."

GROUSE
GROUSE

 Great, fantastic, or awesome.

 "That movie was absolutely grouse!"

GLOSSARY

HEAPS

HEEPS

 A lot or many.

 "There were heaps of people at the festival."

HOW YA GOIN'?

HOW YA GO-IN

 A casual way of asking "How are you?"

 "G'day, Sheila! How ya goin'?"

HOOROO

HOO-ROO

 A casual way to say goodbye.

 "Alright, I'm off now. Hooroo!"

HUNGRY AS A HORSE

 Extremely hungry.

 "I haven't eaten all day, I'm hungry as a horse!"

I RECKON

EYE RECK-ON

 I think or I believe.

 "I reckon it's going to rain this afternoon."

WHAT'S AN AUSSIE'S FAVOURITE TYPE OF MUSIC? HIP-HOP-ER-ROO!

GLOSSARY

JOEY

JO-EE

A baby kangaroo.

"Look at that joey hopping next to its mum!"

JUG

JUG

An electric kettle.

"Can you fill the jug for a cuppa?"

JUMBUCK

JUM-BUK

A sheep.

"The farmer's rounding up his jumbucks."

KICK-OFF

KIK-OFF

The start of a sports game or event.

"The footy match kicks off at 7 tonight."

KOOK

KOOK

An inexperienced or clumsy surfer.

"That guy's such a kook—he keeps wiping out!"

LAMINGTONS

LAM-ING-TUNZ

 Sponge cakes coated in chocolate and coconut.

 "I brought lamingtons for morning tea."

LARRIKIN

LAR-IK-IN

 A mischievous but likeable person.

 "He's such a larrikin, always pulling pranks."

LOLLIES

LOLL-EEZ

 Sweets or candy.

 "I grabbed a bag of lollies for the car trip."

MAD AS A CUT SNAKE

 Very angry or crazy.

 "He was mad as a cut snake when he lost his keys."

MEAT PIE

MEET PI

 A classic Australian savoury pie.

 "You can't watch the footy without a meat pie!"

MOOLAH  MOO-LAH

 Money.

"I can't come out tonight, I'm out of moolah."

MOZZIE MOZ-EE

 A mosquito.

 "Make sure to use repellent, the mozzies are bad tonight."

MUSTER MUS-TUH

 The gathering of cattle or sheep.

 "The drovers are working hard on the muster."

NO DRAMA NO DRAH-MAH

 Same as "no worries" or "it's okay."

 "Thanks for helping me out!" "No drama, mate."

NO WORRIES NO WUR-EEZ

 It's all good; don't stress.

 "Sorry I'm late!" "No worries, happens to everyone."

NIPPERS  NIP-UHZ

 Kids in a junior surf lifesaving program.

 "My son just joined the Nippers at the beach."

67

NOT THE FULL QUID

 Someone who's not very bright or a bit crazy.

 "He's not the full quid if he thinks that'll work."

OUTBACK   OUT-BAK

 Remote inland areas of Australia.

 "They've been travelling through the Outback for weeks."

OZ   OZ

 A short name for Australia.

 "Welcome to Oz, the land of kangaroos!"

PASH   PASH

 A long, passionate kiss.

 "Did you see them having a pash at the party?"

PAVLOVA   PAV-LOH-VUH

 A dessert made of meringue, cream, and fruit.

 "Mum made pavlova for dessert tonight!"

GLOSSARY

PIECE OF PISS
PEESS OV PISS

 Something very easy to do.

 "That exam was a piece of piss, mate."

POSTIE
POHS-TEE

 A postman or mail carrier.

 "The postie dropped off the parcel this morning."

POZZY
POZ-EE

 A good position or spot.

 "Let's grab a pozzy near the stage at the concert."

PREZZY
PREZ-EE

 A present or gift.

 "I'm picking up a birthday prezzy for Mum."

PUB GRUB
PUB GRUB

 Food served at a pub, usually hearty meals.

 "Let's grab some pub grub after the game."

PULL YOUR HEAD IN
PULL YOR HED IN

 A phrase telling someone to stop being silly.

 "Pull your head in, mate, and stop arguing."

QUID

KWID

 A dollar or money in general.

 "I'll lend you twenty quid till payday."

RACK OFF

RACK-OFF

 A rude way to say "go away."

 "If you don't like it, just rack off!"

RAPT

RAPT

 Extremely pleased or happy.

 "I was rapt to hear I got the job!"

RATBAG

RAT-BAG

 A mischievous or unruly person.

 "That little ratbag keeps stealing lollies!"

RASHIE

RASH-EE

 A rash guard shirt worn for sun protection.

 "Don't forget your rashie for the beach, mate."

RIP SNORTER

RIP-SNORT-UH

 Something amazing or fantastic.

 "That was a rip snorter of a goal!"

RIPPER

RIP-UH

 Excellent or fantastic.

 "That was a ripper of a game last night!"

ROCK UP

ROCK UP

 To arrive at a place.

 "She just rocked up to the party uninvited."

ROO

ROO

 A kangaroo.

 "We saw a mob of roos on the way here."

SALTIE

SAWL-TEE

 A saltwater crocodile.

 "Be careful swimming up north; there might be salties."

SANGA

SANG-UH

 A sandwich.

 "I packed a ham and cheese sanga for lunch."

GLOSSARY

SANGER
SANG-UH

 Regional variation of "sanga," meaning sandwich.

 "Grab me a sanger from the cafe, mate."

SAUSAGE SIZZLE
SOS-IJ SIZZ-UHL

 A barbecue fundraiser with sausages served in bread.

 "There's a sausage sizzle at the shops today."

SCRUB
SKRUB

 Bushland or remote countryside.

 "They've been camping out in the scrub."

SERVO
SIR-VOH

 A service station or petrol station.

 "Stop at the servo to grab some fuel."

SHARKY
SHAHR-KEE

 Feeling nervous about sharks in the water.

 "I'm feeling sharky swimming here—it's so deep!"

SHE'LL BE RIGHT
SHEEL BE RAHT

 Everything will be okay or work out fine.

 "Don't stress about the exam; she'll be right."

SHEILA

SHEE-LUH

 A woman.

 "That Sheila over there runs the local cafe."

SHOOT THROUGH

SHOOT THROO

 To leave or disappear quickly.

 "I'm going to shoot through before it gets late."

SHOUT

SHOWT

 To buy a round of drinks for others.

 "It's my shout, so what's everyone having?"

SICKIE

SIK-EE

 A day off work, often taken when not actually sick.

 "I reckon he's chucked a sickie today."

SMOKO

SMOH-KOH

 A short break during work, often for tea or snacks.

 "Time for smoko, let's grab a cuppa."

SNAG

SNAG

 A sausage, often grilled or fried.

 "Throw a couple of snags on the barbie, mate."

GLOSSARY

SPECKY
SPEK-EE

 A spectacular catch, often in Australian Rules football.

 "He took a ripper specky during the game."

SPIT THE DUMMY
SPIT THUH DUM-EE

 To throw a tantrum or overreact.

 "He spat the dummy when he lost the race."

SPRUNG
SPRUNG

 Caught doing something wrong.

 "I got sprung sneaking into the cinema."

STATION
STAY-SHUN

 A large farm or ranch in rural Australia.

 "They run a cattle station out in the Outback."

STIR THE POSSUM
STUR THUH POSS-UM

 To provoke or cause controversy for fun.

 "He's always stirring the possum with his jokes."

STOKED
STOHKD

 Extremely happy or excited.

 "I'm so stoked about the concert this weekend!"

GLOSSARY

STUBBIE
STUB-EE

 A small bottle of beer, usually 375ml.

 "Grab a couple of stubbies from the bottle-o."

SUNBAKE
SUN-BAYK

 To sunbathe.

 "I'm heading to the beach to sunbake today."

SUNNIES
SUN-EEZ

 Sunglasses.

 "Don't forget your sunnies; it's bright out."

SURFIES
SURF-EEZ

 People who surf, often as a lifestyle.

 "The surfies are out catching waves all day."

SWAG
SWAG

 A rolled-up bedroll used for camping.

 "We slept under the stars with just our swag."

SWAGGIE
SWAG-EE

 A swagman or itinerant worker.

 "The old swaggie told us stories by the fire.

TA TA

TAH-TAH

 A casual way to say "bye-bye."

 "Alright, mate, ta ta for now!"

TALL POPPIES

TALL POP-EEZ

 Successful people who are sometimes criticised.

 "He's copped it for being a tall poppy at work."

TEA

TEE

 Dinner or the evening meal.

 "What's for tea tonight? I'm starving!"

TEE-UP

TEE-UP

 To arrange or set something up.

 "I'll tee-up a meeting with the manager."

THONGS

THONGZ

 Flip-flops or sandals.

 "Chuck on your thongs, we're heading to the beach."

TOO RIGHT

TOO RIGHT

 Definitely or absolutely.

 "That was a great game last night!"

GLOSSARY

TRUE BLUE
TROO BLOO

 Genuinely Australian or patriotic.

 "He's a true blue Aussie through and through."

TUCKER
TUK-UH

 Food.

 "There's heaps of tucker at the barbie."

TUCKERBOX
TUK-UH-BOX

 A container for carrying food.

 "Grab the sandwiches from the tuckerbox."

TRY
TRY

 A rugby term for scoring points.

 "He scored a try in the last minute of the game!"

UGG BOOTS
UGG BOOTS

 Sheepskin boots popular for comfort.

 "It's cold, so I'm wearing my Ugg boots today."

UNI
YOU-NEE

 University.

 "I'm starting uni next semester."

UP THE DUFF

UP THUH DUFF

 Pregnant.

 "She just told us she's up the duff!"

VEGGIES

VEJ-EEZ

 Vegetables.

 "Make sure you eat your veggies, mate!"

VEG OUT

VEG OUT

 To relax or unwind, often in front of the TV.

 "I'm going to veg out on the couch tonight."

WALKABOUT

WALK-UH-BOUT

 To wander or go missing.

 "Where's my wallet? It's gone walkabout again!"

WIPEOUT

WIPE-OUT

 Falling off a surfboard or taking a bad fall.

 "That was a gnarly wipeout on that wave!"

WHACKA

WHACK-UH

 A fool or idiot.

"He's such a whacka, forgetting his own keys."

WHINGE
WINJ

To complain, often excessively.

"Stop whinging about the heat, mate!"

WHAT'S CRACKIN'?
WOTS KRACK-IN

A casual greeting meaning "What's happening?"

"G'day, mate! What's crackin'?"

WHAT'S THE GO?
WOTS THUH GO

A casual way to ask "What's happening?"

"What's the go with the plans for tomorrow?"

Y

YAKKA
YAK-UH

Work, often physical labour.

"That was bloody hard yakka today!"

YOU'RE DREAMIN'
YOR DREAM-IN

A response to someone being unrealistic.

"I'm going to win the lottery tomorrow!"   "You're dreamin', mate!"

THANK YOU SO MUCH
FOR MAKING IT THIS FAR!

Thank you so much for picking up my book! I'm thrilled to have been part of your journey into the fun and quirky world of Aussie slang.

If you enjoyed the book *(or even had a laugh or two along the way)*, I'd be incredibly grateful if you could **leave a review on Amazon**. Your feedback not only helps me grow but also helps other readers discover the book.

Here's how you can leave your review:
1. **Open your camera** app on your phone.
2. **Point it** at the QR code below.
3. **Follow the link** to the review page.

SCAN ME

Thanks again, and I hope you have a ripper time mastering Aussie lingo!